Sitting quietly,
doing nothing—Spring comes
and the grass grows.
—*Zen poem*

Doing Nothing

Doing Nothing
coming to the end of
the spiritual
search

STEVEN HARRISON

SENTIENT PUBLICATIONS

First Sentient Publications edition 2008
Copyright © 1997 by Steven Harrison

First published by The Crossroad Publishing Company 1997
Jeremy P. Tarcher/Putnam edition 1998
Jeremy P. Tarcher/Putnam paperback edition 2002

Library of Congress Cataloging-in-Publication Data

Harrison, Steven, 1954-
   Doing nothing : coming to the end of the spiritual search / Steven Harrison. -- 1st
Sentient Publications ed.
     p. cm.
   Originally published: New York : Crossroad, 1997.
   ISBN 978-1-59181-308-8
   1. Spiritual biography-- United States . 2. Nothing (Philosophy) 3. Harrison, Steven,
1954- I. Title.

BL73.H36A3 2007
204'.4--dc22
                                    2007039234

Printed in the United States of America

10 9 8 7 6 5 4 3 2 1

SENTIENT PUBLICATIONS
A Limited Liability Company
1113 Spruce Street
Boulder, CO 80302
www.sentientpublications.com

THIS BOOK IS dedicated to the inquiry that life has presented each of us.

Our accumulation of belief and concept has been accepted, as if it were fact, and added to our already overfilled minds. It has weighed us down almost as much as the neurotic mind we set out to remedy. It is striking how relieved we are when we give up the burden of our acquired spirituality and all its dogma.

There is just as often reaction to the very suggestion that belief creates conflict and that the idea of self, as our core belief, is central to our conflict. There is tremendous attachment to the rituals, religions, and ideologies in which we function and to the psychological center, the "me." There is great difficulty in stepping back from the ideas that we have used for so long to give ourselves a sense of structure and function.

We are both frightened by and attracted to this freedom from our ideas. This churning of relief and anxiety, recognition and reaction, is our collective mind trying to make sense of something it cannot fathom.

The vastness of Life embraces all of this, all of us, in itself, without concern. It is the actuality of Life that we are living, not the conceptual world that our minds generate.

How do we speak to each other without creating authority and power? How do we form relationship that is not bound by fear and need? How do we live in community in a way that expresses communion yet confirms our inherent freedom?

This exploration cannot stop at the deconstruction of the conceptual world and the discord these belief systems have brought about. We need to find what can give expression to the whole in each of our lives, and together, in all of our lives.

Let us each, and together, find out how to live.

Contents

introduction

THIS BOOK IS a work of investigation into the bare actuality of our existence. It was not written for the purpose of creating a particular philosophic or ideated approach to life.

It is not a description of a methodology, or a way to get from confusion to clarity. There is no way, no system, no instruction that will give us certainty in living our lives. Systems, philosophies, beliefs are static, and life is dynamic.

We are already cluttered with conceptualizations. We are taught how to think, how to behave, and how to be. We do not need more instructions on how to live.

This book was not written to be kept on a bookshelf, reread, and quoted. If it is read once, but read thoroughly, with deep reflection, it will serve its purpose.

We are in need not of a new ideology but of the intention and the integrity to look directly at the structures of mind already in existence. We need no one to mediate this view, since it is inherently clear when we are willing to look firsthand at the actuality of our lives.

We can observe directly for ourselves that the basic structure of our reality consists of thought forms arising out of nothing and passing away. There is no observable continuity to this arising-passing away. But there also arises the idea that there is a thinker, a central "me," which is the creator of these thoughts. This "me" is a concept, not an actuality.

This central thought, repetitive, subtle, and usually unconscious, is the core of the reality in which we exist. It is the basis for the entire web of our psychology, social functions, and cosmological and theological beliefs.

The examination of this basic idea of self is the essential beginning of understanding. If this "me" is a thought form, too, and if it also is arising and passing away as all thought appears to do, then who are we? Who is the observer of this passing away of the "me"?

This book is intended to take the reader on a journey through the structure of mind and, perhaps, into the quiet space out of which thought occurs. It leaves some of the work to be done by the reader.

I have no academic credentials, but perhaps this has allowed me the freedom to write what I have written. At a young age I was moved by the pain and discord in the world around and inside me. I was being groomed to be part of a society that seemed to have gone mad. Like many of my generation, I could not reconcile myself to the turmoil of assassinated leaders and war without purpose, nor could I accept the conflict that had become fact in my family, my relationships, and my own mind. Leaving the security of an Ivy League university, I sought to find a complete, final, and universal answer to this pain.

I sought out every mystic, seer, and magician I could find throughout the world. I subjected myself to severe austerities, long periods of isolation, and meditation. I studied the world's philosophies and religions. I spent long periods in India and in the Himalayas, searching, contemplating, being. Throughout the past twenty-five years, I have been a student and teacher of all that I have discovered.

And it was all useless.

No system, philosophy, or religion could address the human condition. Even though I was discovering greater and greater depths of the mind and consciousness, no experience could solve my dilemma. No matter how far I traveled, no matter how intensely I practiced, no matter what master I found, I was still the center of the experience. Every experience, no matter how profound, was collected by the "me." The problem was the collector.

At one point, I went to see a powerful yogi in the Himalayas. I suggested to this man, who had obviously obtained a deep insight into life, that I had come to learn all he knew about the powers of the inner world. His response was simple and to the point: "Why do you want power? What are you afraid of?" Then he walked away.

The exploration of that fear was the beginning and the end of my spiritual journey.

Somewhere in all of this occurred the profound discovery that the problem was not pain and discord but the seeker. The very grasping for an answer, for a response, for a solution that relieved me of the burden of feeling, was the problem. Without the grasping of the seeker, there is no solution. Without a solution, the nature of the problem fundamentally changes.

There is no position, ideology, philosophy, or religion that responds to the question that life poses us. These systems are designed to give us the certainty, solidity, and solace of an answer. The question that life brings us is the movement of life itself, intrinsically dynamic, uncertain, and vital.

For those who have the interest, the fact of existence is present all the time. It may be touched in the quiet, without the distortion of belief. In the face of the vastness, the magic, the unknown quality of life, and in a moment of true humility, we may discover the actuality that washes away all our concepts.

This book is an accounting of this interest, and anything found in it should be tested by the reader's direct contact with who he or she is. This contact comes not with the reading of these words but in the silence that occurs after the words, the thoughts, the "me" pass into nothingness. ❦

a story about absolute truth

A KING WAS ONCE disturbed by the relative appearance of truth. Being an absolute ruler, he decided to do away with relative truth and to enforce absolute truth by decree.

His law was simple. If anyone entered his city and did not tell the absolute truth, they would immediately hang the liar.

He was content that he had found the ultimate expression of truth.

Nearby his kingdom lived a mad mystic, who, upon hearing the king's decree, laughed long and hard.

He presented himself to the king the next day and said, "By your decree, today you will hang me for telling this lie."

The king was stunned. He could not hang the madman for then the mystic would have spoken the truth. Nor could the king not hang him, for then the mystic would have lied.

Instead of doing either, the king gave up his kingdom and went off with the mad mystic to learn the real nature of absolute truth. ❦

something is wrong:
emptiness
and reality

$\mathcal{I}$IT BECOMES EVIDENT to us through the experience of psychological pain that something is wrong. This is the great messenger of life and with it comes a shift in the nature of the world that we know.

Until the message of pain is heard, we are content, dozing creatures of habit, comfort, and dullness. We live in a state of contraction and withdrawal.

The recognition of pain is the moment of freedom. It startles us. We are awake and we hurt. Following this thread of conflict, we may come to the end of our difficulty by coming to the end of our selves.

Perhaps our first attempt will be to dull this pain, or avoid it or deny it. Whatever we do we cannot remove it or escape it. Even if we manage throughout our lives to run from this contact, we will meet our pain at the point of death.

Understanding that we cannot escape, we try to change. We try drugs. We try psychotherapy, meditation, yoga, religion. We try to become something that is free from pain. Yet becoming is the source of pain. The pain is the constant motion to reach for something else, something outside of us that will resolve us, but in fact never does.

We become increasingly spiritual, loving, and altruistic. We live like a demon encased in a saint's clothes. Outwardly, we are happily enlightened, or at least moving satisfactorily on the path to actualization. Inwardly, we are in pain.

Now having prepared and perfected ourselves, and still not finding freedom we become cynical, negating, and motiveless. Still we are becoming, and still we are in pain.

Our entire life is lived relative to this pain, and yet we have never fully felt and embraced our pain. If we embrace it we embrace ourselves, we embrace nothing.

It is this fundamental emptiness that has awakened us to our lives. It is not in fact painful. It is empty. This vast space is the gateway of our reality.

When we talk about emptiness, we are using a word that is inadequate. Perhaps there are no words in English that are useful, because we are not describing a null state. We are describing a very full and complete universe that is simply absent a viewer.

Yet, in this universe, viewing is taking place. Reality, which is the cognition of thought, is occurring. This happens without a thinker. This is emptiness.

Physicists, not metaphysicians, have provided the most elegant attempt at a description of this emptiness. Quantum physicists describe a world of possibility waves with no inherent objectivity or measurability. There is no thingness in this quantum physical world until consciousness enters and creates reality by its observation or contact.

This emptiness does not negate the reality of thought and the cognition of thought. The world does not disappear in this emptiness, it occurs in this emptiness, and it is transformed by the recognition of this emptiness.

We may say that the world is illusion, but it is the viewer that is an illusion. The illusion is that the viewer is constant and solid. The illusion is that the viewer sees an objective world that exists outside its conditioning. That this is illusion and not fact is discernible by simply looking for this viewer. Where is it located? Is it constant? Solid?

The view, without a viewer, arises out of the emptiness. Emptiness is not an abrogation of responsibility in the world. On the contrary, full contact with the world brings full responsibility for the world with it. This is only possible when the notion of a viewer dissolves. Our happiness, our well-being, our integration, cannot be separated from the world's, because we cannot be separated from the world.

Nor is emptiness the nullification of the challenges inherent to life. We must still care for our health, function at work, and relate fully to our family and friends. These challenges now take on a new quality as an expression of this unifying principle. Emptiness introduces us for the first time to the fullness of life.

The viewer is the conceptualization of a continuous thinker. The realization of the absence of a viewer clears the way for the realization of the view.

The view tears apart our conceptual framework and, at the same time, introduces us to the intrinsic reality underlying our ideas. The view fundamentally alters the nature of what we have called emptiness.

Emptiness is a concept that we use relative to our perceived state of fullness, concreteness, and location. This concept is descriptive, but is not what it describes.

What emptiness describes is no more null than we are concrete. What emptiness holds is reality. Reality is the movement of energy itself. Energy is not empty, nor is it concrete. It is dynamic possibility. The view, not the viewer, transforms this dynamic possibility into reality. ℭ

the myth
of
psychology

THE PROFUNDITY OF our contact with our own emptiness is accompanied by the search for explanation. This is the desire to resolve the conflict apparently existent between the solid sense of self and the apparent emptiness we have discovered. The emptiness is interpreted by that self, by thought, as psychological pain.

We are in dangerous territory. We are confused. We turn to a guide for help and that guide is a psychologist, a psychiatrist.

Are we aware that we have made a religious decision? We are trading direct contact with who we are for an explanation based on convention, myth, and social pressures. Are we aware that the therapist's view is to change us? What we are to become is whatever the therapist believes.

We are diagnosed, we are treated, we may even be cured. We may be given drugs, we may be given explanations, therapy, art projects, writing assignments, pillows to scream into, dolphins with which to swim. But what has actually happened?

The self, the center, has been reinforced, the emptiness denied. We are again productive citizens, we are ready to work, reproduce, age, and die. We are still empty, and in between drug dosages, or therapy sessions, we still feel this emptiness as profound pain.

The pain is a messenger. The message is to wake up. Those psychologists and psychiatrists who understand this also understand that they have a fundamentally different function. They become the midwives of consciousness, but only after they have faced their own conflict.

If our lives are concerned with the resolution of this conflict and the discovery of the ultimate truth of our existence, then we must once again embrace this emptiness.

How then do we relate to psychological conflict, the fears, the anxieties, the anger, the unresolved memories of painful and destructive experiences?

When we go to a therapist or a psychologist in response to these conflicted feelings and thoughts, what do we go for?

If we go so that we can continue to function, so that we can get through our lives, so that we can get better, do better, feel better, then perhaps we have gone to the right place.

This is indeed the usefulness of the psychologist, therapist, or psychiatrist. They will apply a bandage. We will function better. Often we will feel as if we have gained great insights into ourselves.

If we cannot make progress, or we are in a crisis, then we can be given drugs. Our state of mind will shift so long as we take the drugs. Typically that shift will be to a more pleasant or functional state of mind. Sometimes the drugs do not work or work in a problematic way.

Sometimes the power of the simple contact with another human being for an hour three times a week is such that we experience an uplifting or expansion of our state. The type of therapy may be irrelevant.

What is deficient with this therapeutic approach to the mind? Nothing, if this modification without fundamental resolution is in fact what we are looking for. There is nothing deficient about therapy, if we recognize there is no end to it and that its purpose is to relieve the pressure of our conflict so that we can function normally. Is the "normal" that is being described to us what we want to be?

∾

THE CONCERNED MAN brings a chicken to the psychiatrist, saying, "Doctor, it is my brother, he thinks he is a chicken."

Does the doctor treat the concerned man's brother? What treatment would be effective? How many sessions will it take for the brother to break through the delusionary state?

Isn't it clear that nothing will be effective in the treatment because the premise is wrong?

When mind looks to itself to resolve its own conflict, can it be done? Or is the premise wrong?

For many, the approach to the problem with the brother who thinks he is a chicken is entirely different. They have recognized that this is not the brother, but a chicken. To resolve the conflict, they seek a different order of authority, more exotic. If the psychiatrist cannot help, then perhaps a veterinarian will do it. It is a chicken after all.

Catholics seek answers in Hinduism, Jews in Buddhism, atheists in existentialism, communists in capitalism. Americans go to India. Indians go to America. If this does not solve the problem, then that will. If the psychiatrist did not help my brother, then the veterinarian will.

But still the premise is wrong, and no matter where we go, or whom we ask, the conflict continues.

To whom then does the concerned man go to help his poor brother who thinks he is a chicken?

Whom do we go to in order to resolve our own conflicts?

Is it not clear that the premise of our conflict must be understood before we can hope to know how to resolve it? After all, there really is no brother, so there is no reason for resolution of the brother's delusion that he is a chicken. Yet there is conflict.

The mind is a self-created web of neuroses with the appearance of conflict, not unlike the brother's delusion that he is a chicken.

The brother's delusion does not exist, because the brother does not exist. Our conflict does not exist, because we do not exist.

Without the center, is there conflict?

THE MODEL OF the mind in medicine has changed in the last half-century. It is now generally accepted that the mind is easily manipulated by mechanical means, in particular, drugs and surgery.

Science recognizes that it does not know enough about the biochemistry of the mind to put in place a unified theory of the mind's functions. But science operates under the assumption that this is just a matter of time and the progression of scientific knowledge.

In lockstep with this model of mind, the model of psychiatric care has begun to view much of its work to be the discovery of appropriate alterations of brain chemistry.

There is an undeniable cause and effect in the chemical manipulation of the brain. The psychotic becomes docile with Thorazine, the depressive becomes content with Prozac.

What this model of mind and psychiatry is missing—and it is a large hole—is the view of the context of the mind. Because the mind is seen as a mechanical process that exists in the individual and in isolation from its context, psychiatry cannot address the larger picture. This is because science does not have a larger picture.

As astounding as it appears, science does not have any model of consciousness. There is no working, unified theory of consciousness in science. This is the case even though consciousness is the context in which the mind, and all of its permutations—including science and psychiatry—are taking place.

There is no fundamental resolution in the therapeutic world. There never has been.

If we are interested in resolution of psychological conflict, we must look elsewhere.

First, we must look at the function of psychological time in the perpetuation of psychological structures. Without the idea of time, there cannot be the idea of "getting better," or "working on it," or "processing," or any of the myriad notions of psychological progression. Without the concept of time, there is only one thing occurring. It is occurring in the present and it is evident for us to see, if we wish to do so, without the help of an intermediary.

Without psychological time, the contact with psychological conflict, and the resulting understanding and resolution of that conflict, occurs only in the present.

Secondly, we must look at psychological memory, which as an aspect of thought, creates the history of events not as they happened, but as they happened to us. This inclusion of the subject in the history, and the continuous calling forth of this subject with the history, and the projection of this subject-with-the-history as the future, is the basis of psychological conflict.

Fully understanding the interaction of these two aspects of thought—time and memory—brings psychological conflict into the accessible and immediate present. There is no place else.

Now that we have the conflict in the immediate present, what do we do with it?

Absolutely nothing.

To do anything in relationship to the conflict is to give it substance or energy. To attempt to approach it, to manipulate it, to make it better, to make it go away, simply entrenches this conflict in the realm of our reality. We have reinforced it by positing its resolution. We have created further conflict when that resolution does not occur.

If we do nothing, what occurs? Nothing occurs. The conflict has no one to claim it. It has no energy. It has no opposite. It can no longer exist. It is no longer an aspect of our reality.

This is the resolution of psychological conflict. It takes place only in the moment. It does not require anyone's help. It does not require anything of us but our silence. ❧

the myth
of
enlightenment

WE HAVE SEEN the limitation, and perhaps, the destructiveness of the psychological model, but we still are driven to understand.

This need to resolve the contact with our own emptiness may become distorted by the mythology of enlightenment.

We are told that the resolution to the contact we have made with emptiness is elsewhere, is a state, a place called enlightenment.

This mythology appears instantly to cure us of this emptiness, because it instantly fills us with concepts. We have a purpose, a goal, a struggle, a journey, a direction. We are no longer empty, but we are still looking for the cure for our emptiness.

We are full, we have lost contact with our emptiness, but it is remembered and projected in thought.

We will spend a great deal of time looking for this enlightenment. But, looking is useless, because it is not there.

We can sit on cushions facing walls, dance in ecstasy, pray, chant. We can travel the world looking for this enlightenment. We can find the greatest of gurus and the most secret of doctrines. It is useless.

We can even realize that it is useless. In our cleverness, we can realize that it is not there, it is here.

It has always been here. It is in the moment.

It is not.

It is not here. It is not anywhere. Enlightenment is a concept, an idea, a belief.

The self, the "me," has projected its own end out there, or in here, but it has projected in time. In time, we are always approaching, never still.

Enlightenment is a myth because the self is a myth.

We are back in contact with our emptiness. ❧

teachers:
authority, fascism,
and love

THE SEEKER, AFTER a long and difficult journey and many hardships, reaches the mountaintop where resides the guru in solitude. "What, master, is the meaning of life?" the supplicant asks.

"Life, my son, is a bowl of cherries," replies the guru.

The seeker is outraged after all he has been through to reach the guru and lets the guru know what he thinks of his answer.

The guru considers for a moment, and says, "You mean it's not?"

☙

WE ARE SO disoriented, confused by our emptiness that we look for someone who is not that way.

We hear that there are teachers, gurus, special people with power and insight.

Maybe there are, but why are we looking for them?

Is this movement the reaction to chaos and the search for authority, for direction, the embrace of fascism in the face of unrest? If so, we know that the authority we find will solve our problem. We also know that the authority we find will then become our problem.

This teacher is our projection, the reflection of our fear, anxiety, and laziness. We project a father figure who is certain, authoritative, and disciplined. We project a mother figure who is nurturing, forgiving, and uncritical.

We empower the teacher, but we never allow ourselves intimacy. We do not want to acknowledge who the teacher is, but in fact we already know.

This teacher is us. The father is the child. The child is the father. By accepting our collective projections, the teacher accepts our control. We have created an authority to which we bow, but we control this authority. We know the emperor has no clothes, but we will not say a word so long as our needs are met.

This guru game is like the enlightenment game, we play it because we do not want to face our emptiness.

We have misunderstood our confusion when we think there is an answer to it. The confusion is not a result of questions that are too hard, but rather a questioner who is disintegrating. Confusion is the introduction to true intelligence. This is an intelligence without a center and without the dominance of thought.

If we sacrifice that intelligence in the name of the guru, if we put aside our spiritual responsibility for the authority of another, we have entered the realm of lost souls. Beware all those who enter here. The souls are lost. The guru is lost.

Power is corruption. There is abundant evidence in the sex and money scandals of a multitude of gurus that this is the case. How many insightful and charismatic teachers have become mired in intrigue and deception as their followers rationalize their leader's behavior? The movement to increasing stupidity is the very nature of this structure, because the first step, the abdication of responsibility, is a misstep.

No authority can answer our question, but perhaps we will be fortunate and discover someone who will question our answer.

This gift of the question is a most precious thing. If we come upon such a giver, and if we are receptive and humble enough to recognize this meeting, we have entered into a fundamentally different kind of relationship.

There is no authority, no power in this relationship other than the authority and power of the question.

Where the question is present, there is no place for an answer to rest. Without an answer, there is no power, no authority, no answerer.

Our projection onto this guru cannot find a place to reside. When we meet such a person, and we are given the question, we realize there is nothing we will acquire. We are in relationship with nothing to get and everything to give. We are in love. This is the guru. We have met our true nature. ℭ

the dark night
of
the soul

WHAT OCCURS WHEN there is no psychologist, no guru, no god to help us? What occurs when there is no resolution to our conflict, no enlightenment, no end to our sorrow? What occurs when there is only emptiness and nothing to fill it? Our world, our life, our relationships collapse. We collapse.

This collapse of our identity and the impossibility of escape from that collapse is the end and the beginning. This "dark night of the soul," through which nothing can pass, is not an event, not an enlightenment. It is not in time or of time. It is not about us, or becoming something other. It is not causal, not the result of anything.

No one can take us to this or through this. And we cannot create it, hurry it, or end it. It is a moment, a lifetime.

Having been reduced to nothing, nothing may then express itself. This expression of nothingness is love. Love is without a source and without an object, it has always been present. ☙

doing
nothing

THE IDEA OF meditation may attract us for many reasons.

Perhaps it is because of our overwhelming neuroses, the heaviness of constant thought, the pressure we feel, the anxiousness and stress of our lives.

Perhaps it is some faint nostalgia for a state of rest we vaguely remember, a state of rest to which we can no longer find our way.

It may be an interest directed by our need for control. It may be an extension of the quest for power.

We have become interested in meditation through despair, depression, tragedy, or death. We want to find God.

By implication, all of these approaches to meditation are looking for something other.

It is this fundamental acquisitiveness, and the movement of dissatisfaction with what we are and where we are that brings us to meditation.

It should not be surprising then that meditation becomes the hunt for experiences. The mind that is dissatisfied with its life is dissatisfied with itself and looks for this other.

There is a state of bliss, a state of peace, a state of love that it hunts for, a state that will be different, better, more complete than the mind which is hunting.

And yet, the field in which the mind hunts for this other, is the mind itself.

Finding nothing but itself, the mind, the meditator, looks for significance in what it finds. It finds experiences, states, gods and demons. From this it creates descriptions, explanations, and instructions. From this are created philosophy and religion. Now meditation can be conditioned. The search can have a definite discovery of an already-described experience.

The mind has folded into itself. It has discovered a self-created truth and yet is still contained within itself.

If we are told to sit, close our eyes and look for the white light, we will create that white light. Or Buddha. Or Shiva. Or Jesus.

This is interesting in its own way. We can be educated or conditioned to experience particular phenomena in our meditation.

It can appear to be a joyful experience to find our god in meditation. But where did our god come from? Is this not a projection of the same mind that is in profound conflict? Isn't our god, the serene and compassionate one, an expression of this conflict? By creating this being of light, do we not imply that we exist in the shadows, that we are not that? Are we not still in conflict?

The word "love" is not love, the word "god" is not god. Can we understand that these words "love" and "god" by their nature create an other, a separation? Once this separation exists unconsciously, then the "me" looks for "god" or "love," but can never have it. It is only through the dissolution of the concept, that is the idea of "love" and the idea of "me" that real love is found. This is not the "love" described by words, but by silence.

The question is often asked, "How do we approach our minds?" This question has no answer.

From the questioner's perspective, we are the mind. We need not approach since we are already there.

The question is often asked, "How do we go beyond our minds?" The question presumes that we will still be there observing it all when "beyond" is reached. Beyond the mind means beyond the questioner, so who will be there to observe?

But, perhaps the questions of approaching the mind and going beyond the mind are really the same question.

Mind after all is what we live every day. It is our thoughts, feelings, ideas, motivations, strategies, fears, attractions, dreams. It is this apparently complex and interwoven nexus of thought that we call "me." We find this "me" located in a physical body and our lives are about the protection and advancement of this me/body.

Through social agreements handed down from parent to child, teacher to student, government to citizen, priest to parishioner, thought expands its depth and breadth and consequently gains the appearance of substance. The very movement of genetic material from generation to generation is the movement of thought and memory, and this conditions us collectively and individually.

We do not live lives of originality and discovery, but rather lives echoing the perspectives we have inherited.

The most fundamental conditioning is that of "I am," the basic sense of self-centeredness. This is the sense that there is a thinker who thinks thoughts and who somehow lives in our bodies. This is the illusion that we have location.

Quantum physicists agree that in the subatomic universe objects exist in quantum nonseparability. Quantum objects are not located, they are not separate. Once having acted on another object, the objects continue to be connected. This connectedness is unaffected by distance, because the connecting force does not move through space. Close and far are the same in this regard.

While this is not a model of consciousness per se, it is an indication of how the sense of location, autonomy, and separation which is apparent is not the case at all.

Yet our sense of location and separability is so ingrained in the collective human psyche that it is accepted as the basis of our reality. Those who have tried to concentrate their mind, silence their mind, or simply sit still, know directly that no thinker is controlling anything.

This thinker's residence in the body becomes suspect every night when we fall asleep and find a substantially different reality occurring, often waking with the feeling of returning to our bodies. It is a wonder that there is such concreteness to our sense of "me." And yet it is so.

How then do we see that which we are, but which has been distorted by our conditioning? Any approach to ourselves is from ourselves and is consequently part of the conditioning. It is a hopeless dilemma, and there is nothing we can do about it.

So, can we do nothing? A simple thing: nothing. There is a fundamental quiet in nothing.

Let us try it and see. Stop right now and do nothing.

๑

As IT TURNS out, nothing is a surprisingly active place, but it is here that we may discover what we are. In the resistance to doing nothing, the fear of doing nothing, of being nothing, we begin to discover the parameters of the self.

Sit in a room for one week and do nothing. What will happen to us? Will we die from it? Will we become insane? Why does such a thing as doing nothing cause such fear?

Doing nothing outlines the doer in an unmistakable way. If we wish to approach our mind, the most direct way is to do nothing. If we want to go beyond our mind, do nothing.

☙

PERHAPS WHAT BECOMES most clear when we do nothing is that thought keeps on going, as though we were doing something. There is great humor in this. There is no on/off switch to thought. We are sure that we are the thinker of these thoughts, but they seem to have a mind of their own.

But if these thoughts do have a mind of their own, then who is the thinker? And more important, where is this thinker, this "me"?

The most fascinating thing is that we cannot find the thinker anywhere. Thoughts are coming and going, feelings, images, plans, dreams, fears and even commentaries on these thoughts are occurring. But, we cannot find the thinker in the nothingness anywhere. Just thought.

The body will begin aching and hurting as we sit doing nothing. The attention is drawn from thinking to the body, and suddenly this density appears to be the thinker, the body is the "me."

But, let us look at this. Does this body have any more continuity than the thoughts we were just observing? The aches and pains of the body, as the body does nothing, seem to happen on their own and pass away on their own, much like the thoughts.

Let us find our center in the body where the "me" resides. Where is it that we are when we observe the world about us? Where are we located, actually?

There is an interesting thing that occurs when this question is asked. Closely observe where the center is felt to be. Now, having located where we "are" in our body, and having found this location, from where do we observe this location in our body? And from where do we observe that observation point? Following this, can we really find anything solid or continuous, in fact? Where is the thinker, the observer, the doer located?

Our entire reality is built upon a premise of a "me" located in our body. Perhaps it is time to look again. ℒ

concentration,

meditation,

and space

WHAT IS THE nature of meditation when using techniques?

Through the use of meditation techniques, one can concentrate the mind. A concentrated mind focuses on one image, sound, or thought.

The value of this is limited. In relationship to the discovery of ultimate truth, concentration of the mind is irrelevant.

By bringing our mind back to the object of concentration, over and over again, we become less agitated. We bring our mind back to our breath, or back to our mantra, or back to our visualization. Now our mind has only the breath, only the mantra, only the visualization.

This is not quiet, this is dullness. We are concentrated, but we have lost our sensitivity. We are training ourselves not to pay attention, we are hypnotizing ourselves, putting ourselves back to sleep before we have even awakened.

What is it that we are trying to achieve with this concentration? What is it that we are moving away from? What is it that causes the fragmentation in which we live, to which we respond by trying so desperately to focus ourselves?

The essential structure of identification is unchanged in a concentrated mind. The "me" is now concentrated, focused, if anything it is more powerful and entrenched.

The problem of life is not whether the mind is concentrated or not, it is resolving the question of who is doing the thinking.

It is also possible through meditation techniques to cultivate a mind which is without apparent thought, or which exists in bliss or some otherwise altered state. But is this mind free from division and conflict? Does restructuring our mind through repetition, privation, or other dulling techniques create true freedom?

What is the nature of the being who so desperately wants to change? We are trying to change into something else. What is this something? Is it new, or is this something we want to change into a description we have inherited, or come to believe in, or been convinced we should be?

Our fundamental dissatisfaction projects itself into a mirror image. We create a kind of alter ego state, a state that we are to become. Now the fragmented, neurotic mind projects concentration and focus. We sit compulsively in order to concentrate. We haughtily describe our inner work to others. We use the relative power that comes from a concentrated mind to impress others, to gain position or security. The mind is concentrated, but the fundamental neurosis has simply expanded.

The deeper one goes into restructuring the mind, the more expanded the neurosis and the illusion become. We can even create a god and lose ourselves in that god. But, that god is the self, the mind, the "me," and it is in conflict.

Techniques used to alter the mind or concentrate it cannot be of help if we want to find out what is beyond the self. They may have value in the exploration of thought, they may be useful in dealing with psychological issues, and they may be of use in modifying the symptoms of physical illness. But they cannot take the self beyond itself.

What is the nature of meditation without techniques?

Can we bring awareness to the moment, whatever its content? This is the cultivation of awareness, bringing the attention to the moment over and over until there is a constant consciousness. This awareness without comment, without discrimination, without judgment is often taught as the end result of certain spiritual practices. But in actuality, this is a state of mind, a stance, a position requiring a watcher who is "aware." In fact, this watcher is not in real contact with anything.

This state of apparent awareness is a kind of virtual reality created by thought as an approximation of what pure consciousness might be like. After we have spent a great deal of time sitting in empty rooms "paying attention," a zombiesque quality emerges. This awareness is generally addicted to quiet or otherwise controlled spaces and lacks what might be described as intelligence. This lack of intelligence means that this so-called awareness cannot change or adapt as the situation of life changes. It can only be "aware," that is aloof, distant and uninvolved.

Since this cultivation of awareness takes place in a context—that is, with a teacher, or a spiritual school, or meditative or religious framework—the awareness becomes conditioned by the context.

It is often the case that we are attracted to the cultivation of awareness or other no-technique techniques because we are overwhelmed by our lives. We have been unable to control our lives and seek to distance ourselves from our own existence.

The problem is that the conflict is in the watcher, the one who is aware, not the objects of our awareness. Our lives *are* out of control. What happens if we don't distance ourselves from that fact?

This fundamental contact with the chaos of what we are, what we think, is very important. Without anything to buffer us from this contact, our world is unified. With this contact, there is only one thing happening.

This unification changes us, it is the expression of change.

Awareness is not the result of anything. There is nothing that causes it. There is nothing we can do to create it.

We have seen the limitation of techniques and of nontechniques in meditation. Without meditation or meditation techniques, then in actuality, what is there?

Thought arises and passes. Awareness exists. The thinker does not. Sitting without intention, we may enter the space between thoughts and discover our true nature.

Thought may try to describe this space, but it cannot. This space is without thought, and consequently without the "me." The fact is that we cannot approach this space volitionally or intentionally. There is no technique, philosophy, instruction, or religion that will help us experience silence. Everything that we acquire as help is in the way because the inquirer is in the way.

And yet, nothing is in the way because although the "me" likes to consider itself substantive, solid, and continuous, in fact there is no "me" that can be found. There is nothing obstructing silence, and there is nothing to do to find this silence. It is already present, waiting for us to cease trying.

So much energy goes into the looking for, the grasping for. Simply stop. ℭ

the nature
of
thought

THOUGHT IS WHAT arises from the background of quiet in the field of consciousness. Thought may take the form of what we call emotion or feeling, it may take the form of concept or idea, it may be holographic or symbolic. Thought has the capacity to create past and future.

Thought cannot take form without an object and subject. Thought cannot take form without time. Thought cannot experience anything directly. Thought cannot be aware of itself.

Thought is reality. Without thought, there is no reality. This thought-reality is not actual and has no inherent thingness or substance.

What is undivided only appears to be divided by thought. Thought separates into this or that. Thought cannot contain unity, because there is always what is outside of thought. Unity contains thought because unity contains everything.

Thought implies a thinker. A thinker has thoughts. Thoughts may be observed. The thinker cannot be observed, other than as thought.

Thought constricts or limits. Consciousness is limitless. Thought requires consciousness. Consciousness does not require thought. ℰ

language
and
reality

For all the years of her young life, Sally had never spoken a word. Her mother had taken her to all the specialists, but to no avail.

One morning at breakfast, Sally threw her toast down and exclaimed, "This toast is burned. I can't eat this!"

Her mother was overwhelmed.

"Sally, you're talking!" she said, "Why have you never spoken before in all these years?"

And Sally said, "Everything has been all right up to now."

UNDERSTANDING LANGUAGE is integral to understanding thought and reality.

As we observe the nature of what we are, we also describe the observation. This naming process is necessary for us to function in the world. It is what a child learns as it grows with the primary learning being the difference between "me" and "not me." The use of language or naming is the very thing that differentiates objects, actions, and qualities in the world. This distinction or separation is the basis of intellect and consequently the basis for the apparent manipulation of the world around us. It is not however, the basis for true intelligence.

What is lost in the learning of differentiation is the underlying unity from which this world of names and of separate objects grew. As the "me" center is established and the world that appears to be outside of "me" is learned and described through language, the actuality of the undifferentiated prelinguistic nature of life is forgotten.

Language, which was originally a representation of an aspect of a whole, concretizes into its own reality. As language develops, it is used not only to name these "now-real" objects, but also to describe their relationship to each other.

While we may originate in a prelinguistic state, we soon learn the difference between "tree" and "house." We learn the difference between "big house" and "small house." We learn the difference between "your big house" and "my small house."

Somewhere, language and concept jump from the concrete-object-oriented word to the abstract. Now we "want your big house," we do not "like my small house." We have a "problem" with the small house. We will only be "fulfilled" with the big house. Language describes all of these objects and relationships. We forget that this is only language, word, thought. Where does the "problem" actually exist?

We have lost the stillness of the undifferentiated world of the prelinguistic state.

Implicit in the development of language is the "me" and the "me-object" relationship. There is no named without a namer, and no namer without a named. As language develops, we are swallowed by the reality that language creates.

The identification with the "me-object" relationship as the basis of our reality is also the basis of our pain. While we may crave the wholeness that we experienced before language, we cannot find that unity in the world we have created through language. Now we can only approximate this unity with language. Rather than rediscovering the underlying, prelinguistic wholeness that we have layered over, we settle for more language.

We create elaborate descriptions of unity, we create symbolic representations of unity, we discover archetypal symbols of unity. We create psychology, philosophy, and religion. But, because we are still looking within the realm of language and its inherent me-object structure, we never actually come to wholeness.

We are faced with a profound paradox. How does the search for understanding transcend itself? We can see that the search itself is a block to the comprehension of wholeness, because the searcher, by nature, objectifies and divides the world.

If we withdraw into prelingualism, we have withdrawn from the "me-object" reality. We can experience only an apparent unity here, because we fear and exclude the objective world. Now we have created a subjective world, with no objects. We no longer function, we are autistic, withdrawn. Denial of the conditioned reality is not useful, because it does not allow integration.

We can only address this question within the context of the objective reality. By standing back from reality, our freedom is limited by our dissociation and fear of contact. We truly live in this relative world only when we have an intelligence that transcends division. This intelligence must be based on both a recognition of the nature and limitations of the relative "me-object" relationship and the underlying unity, which is its wellspring.

The amalgam of subjective and objective worlds includes the whole of life, a life into which we merge. Without the constriction of a viewer, the view has expanded without limitation. The viewer can only exist in the relative reality, the view can only be from unity. ℰ

religion, symbols, and power

THE LITTLE BOY was drawing when his mother noticed and asked, "What are you drawing, Jimmy?"

The little boy, without looking up, answered, "A picture of God."

"But, Jimmy," his mother replied, "Nobody knows what God looks like."

"They will once I'm finished."

෨

THAT WHICH IS not thought, silence, has no language and is consequently unknown. Humankind has never liked what it could not know, explain, and thereby control.

Faced with this dilemma, we created religion.

Religion has always explained the unknown in knowable terms and has created symbols for that which could not be known. This symbology is so deeply imbedded in our minds, cultures, and cosmology that it is rarely questioned from inside the religious paradigms. From outside that paradigm, the religious imagery loses its impact, its subliminal meaning.

The Christian cannot see God in the figure of Kali, fangs dripping with blood, her necklace made of skulls, dancing on a corpse. The Hindu cannot see God in a man nailed bleeding and in agony on a cross. We can only see God if we have been indoctrinated. God is a learned symbol.

Friedrich Nietzsche asked the obvious question: "Which is it—is man one of God's blunders or is God one of man's blunders?"

Most importantly, religion functions to relieve the anxiety of the absolute fact for each of us that we will die, that our family will die, that our friends will die. Religion promises us that although we may die, we will continue. And, if we believe, then our afterlife will be glorious.

The repetition of religious ritual reassures us about death in a way that nothing else does, and it is the public, collective nature of these rituals that is so powerful. The group ritual enhances our sense of well-being, of connection, of safety. But, is this effect actual and transformative, or does it merely metaphorically represent the underlying reality that we have yet to absorb? Have we settled for the mechanical, habitual repetition of ritual, when what we need is authentic mystical union?

Do we become addicted to ritual, to religion? Has the death anxiety been relieved or understood, or has it simply been masked? We have to go deeper than blind ritual to fully resolve our fear of death.

Religion has come to have another function over the aeons, which is to control the behavior of the populace and order society. Religion, because of the deeply ingrained symbols, has tremendous power over its populace.

The development of religious conscience conditions the society, and may restrict the expression of primitive and destructive behaviors by proscribing a way of living and acting. This in itself is not the problem.

The problem that grows out of the religious conscience is the division of our world. This is the inner division of our impulses, desires, and aggressions juxtaposed with the conditioned behavior of our religion. Out of religious conscience, we have produced rote behavior motivated by guilt. H.L. Mencken called conscience "the inner voice which warns us that someone may be watching."

We have divided ourselves. The "good" person is our religious behavior, which can express itself publicly. The "bad" person must remain hidden and can only express itself in furtive ways.

Outwardly, the effect of religious conscience, and the behavior that comes from it, is conflict among religions. After all, if our religious behavior is the expression of moral rectitude, then all other religious expressions become, at best, misguided. At worst, the differences become the rationale for bigotry, violence, and war.

We are attracted to the moral force of religious belief because it describes with such paternalistic certainty, the details of how to live. This surety of what to do that religion brings with it also contains a surety of what not to do.

Juxtaposed, the absolute certainty of two religions can only create conflict. One has to be wrong, and that one must always be the other.

The Quakers say it well in their unique, simple style, "All the world is queer except me and thee; and sometimes I think thee is a little queer."

The control of society through the modification of behavior is the measure of the power of religion. And, as always with power, there are power brokers—the priesthood.

These are the interpreters of the law, the representation of God himself. They speak for the silence, and this is where distortion takes place. Silence does not require a spokesperson.

Religion has, by its nature, created division in the world. It is the greatest of ironies that wars are fought over religion. Religion has brought us the concepts of sin and hell in the West and of acceptance of poverty and injustice in the East. Religion, as a basis for culture, is a force of fragmentation.

Yet, religion reflects something profoundly important and common to us all. It is the exoteric formulation of what is hidden inside us. But, it is only the beginning.

Why do we seek solace in the exoteric without the sublime realization of the esoteric? Without this direct realization, the rituals of religion are unconscious echoes of our collective, historic understanding. The ritual brings this history to the present. We experience, through the conditioning of the religion, the qualities associated with the history of that religion, repeated over and over. The repetition brings with it feelings of familiarity and security.

The exoteric, organized religious form has nothing more to offer than the repetition of these historic, ritualized qualities—unless we go deeper.

∽

A GREAT RABBI died and left his spiritual work to his son to carry on.

The son was a great man in his own right, but he did the work of a rabbi in a completely different manner than his father.

The people who had become used to the father's ways came to the son.

"You are not doing what your father did," they complained.

The son replied, "But indeed I am. He imitated no one and I am imitating no one."

∽

AT THE HISTORIC core of every religion is not ritual, but someone who broke through ritual to direct

contact with the transcendental. They were not following religion. They were discovering it and living
it. Moses, Jesus, Buddha, Lao-tzu, Mohammed were
not following anything but the expression of their
direct contact with the actuality of life.

But we follow them, not our own direct contact
with life. In fact, we follow merely the ritual that
represents these mythic figures and we follow the
religious hierarchy that controls these rituals.

ᴏ

A MAN BOARDED a train for Delhi and sat across from a
swami. The swami was uttering all sorts of incanta-
tions and taking dust from a bag and throwing it
into the air. Unable to suppress his curiosity, the man
finally asked the swami what he was doing.

"I am protecting this railcar from tigers with
my special tiger dust," replied the swami.

"But," the man protested, "there aren't any
tigers within a thousand miles of us!"

And the swami said, "Effective, isn't it?"

ᴏ

IT IS THE RITUALISTIC nature of all religion that is most
interesting. The inherent promise of all religion is

that the adherence to a prescribed methodology, the enactment of particular rituals, the practice of certain customs will bring about the result of heaven, god-realization, enlightenment, or whatever version of certainty a particular religion embodies.

This religious or ritualistic mind is innate to the human psyche. Religion is not the invention of thought. It is thought's inherent expression.

Thought is faced with a vastness, a universal energy that it cannot control, understand, or even touch. In this recognition, thought can fall silent.

Or it can try to find patterns relating the thought–behavior and the surrounding world. This is the ritualistic mind. It is the basis of behavior and personality. It believes, in a religious way, that its behavior affects the world around it.

The truth can be seen from the mind that is silent. The behavior and the world which behavior seeks to affect are the very same thought. Without the illusion of a thinker, this thought is laid bare. This is the end of the religious mind and the end of ritual.

The universe is not actually divided into thoughts and a thinker. Thought does not affect the world through ritualistic behavior. By collapsing this construct into the single actuality, the actuality can be seen. There is the spontaneous movement of thought, which projects a thinker, a behavior, a world to be affected, a god to respond. This is reality, reality is thought.

Looking directly at the nature of the religious mind is difficult for a religiously inclined person. How can the question "What is religion?" approach religious faith without a reaction? Can this faith absorb such a question, or must it protect its structure by cutting off the question or reacting to the questioner?

The faith we are talking about is not faith, but belief. If we believe the sun rises in the east, we can entertain challenge to this belief, because it is based in truth. But if we believe the sun rises in the west, then the challenge to our belief is also to everything we have built around it. We cannot bear the challenge to our entire belief structure, so we cut off with reaction, dismissal, and avoidance. Reaction can never see itself. It has its own rationale for its existence. Reaction calls itself "faith," and says, "I have faith that the sun rises in the west."

A simple observation would show that the sun does not rise in the west. What explanation could possibly be heard by those who believe the sun does rise in the west?

Perhaps all that can be said is, "See for your-self. The sun is rising."

Belief can never be authenticated. It can be defended through reaction, it can be strengthened through conditioning, it can be expanded through coercion, but belief can never know if it is true or not. Belief can never take the risk that it will find out that it is, in fact, false.

This inherent insecurity is why belief is so destructive and has historically made religion one of the great sources of conflict.

Faith is what results from belief allowing itself to be questioned, examined, tested. When belief is placed in that fire, the impurities are burned off and what is left is faith.

Faith is not afraid of questions or challenge. It is not concerned with convincing. Faith is absolute. It is the substratum of the relative world of belief.

Faith is what is left when what can be stripped away, is. In that, what we come to is not faith in the divine, rather what we come to is the divine.

By questioning our beliefs, will we find this faith? The only thing we will get by questioning our beliefs is very tired. It is not being suggested that we acquire a new belief about finding faith by questioning.

It is not a mechanical process by which we get from belief to faith in ten easy steps. It is not an intellectual process of methodically questioning.

Faith is not lost, and so does not need to be found. ℭ

the crisis
of
change

CRISIS IS THE resistance to change. Change is the nature of our existence. Thought, embodied in the "me," is static because it can only approximate life. Change, which is movement, is dynamic and is a threat to the dominance of thought. Change contradicts thought and its center, the "me."

Can we embrace change and understand that it releases us from the endless repetition of thought and conditioning? Change is the only exit from our selves. Without this embrace, we will experience the awakening of our own true nature not as change but as crisis. Without this embrace, we will be left with just our resistance and reaction.

The dominance of thought is so great that the "me-center" will form around this reaction of resistance. Even if the mind can no longer function, and the body's health breaks down, the center, the "me," will not let go.

At the depth of crisis, we will try to make a deal. If we are allowed to survive, if we pull through, then things will be different. We will be better, nicer, more honest.

This deal is not made with the devil. The deal is made with ourselves. We have created the crisis. We are negotiating its end. When it ceases, we will continue as before. We will not change, because we cannot change.

We are static, repetitive habits—the endless repetition of the thought, "I am."

Change is dynamic. We are static. We cannot change, we can only resist change. We resist out of fear.

We try to construct our life, our relationships, our work, our families so that we can predict and control them. We discover over and over that this is impossible. We struggle harder and harder. The discovery that this control of life is impossible becomes an ever-increasing crisis.

Still, we struggle to control change. We want what is dynamic and free, what is arising spontaneously and passing away, what is impermanent to be static and controllable. But, life is not that way.

Fear is what drives this center and what it fears is its own cessation. But, the fact is there is nothing to fear, because there is nothing to cease. The crisis is over because there is nothing left to resist. Change is the movement of energy without hindrance. It is the echo of life itself.

Change moves through us, through our habits, our resistance, our denial. Change is the truth of life.

We can observe this directly, without help, without interpretation. There is nothing that we can find that stays the same.

Each thought occurs and then decays. Each structure that expresses out of thought—our body, our family, our work, our society—also changes as it manifests. We cannot stop this change.

Is there anything that we can find which does not change?

Only thought believes otherwise. Thought is incapable of perceiving the evanescence of reality, because thought is reality and cannot observe its own nature.

Our identification with this mental blind spot, this idea that life must be controlled, means that we have lost contact with change. We have lost contact with our true nature.

Change is freedom. It is the end of attachment. It is the end of fear. There is nothing that binds us, there never has been. ℒ

reaction, projection, and madness

THE STRUCTURE OF thought has evolved to a complexity that cannot be reproduced by the most advanced computers. This structure, because of its intricacy and speed, has come to look and feel like it is solid, continuous, and substantial. Thought has become self-referential, putting itself into the equation when calculating its perceptions, thoughts, and feelings.

Thought projects this sense of solidity into the apparent world, and projects the qualities of its own thought fragments as that world.

These qualities, projected, make up the universe in which we move. The world then fulfills the prophecy of our mind's perspective, because the world is our mind.

Mind is not simply the thoughts of which we are aware and with which we identify. Mind is also the collective, the unconscious, the historic, the genetic—the whole of humankind's conditioning.

When we see a man or a woman, we look with the eyes of an ape, of a hunter-gatherer, of a preliterate serf, of a worker in the new factories of the industrial revolution, of a politically correct denizen of the twentieth century. All these eyes are our eyes. We see from history, from memory, from conditioning.

Our education, our culture, our language is built upon the thoughts and memory of history counted in thousands of years. Our biological memory, our genetic makeup is built upon uncountable millennia of thought.

This accumulation of knowledge, information, memory is assimilated in an ever more frenetic thought process. Outside this collective web of thought there is no Christian, Jew, or Moslem. There is no man or woman. No white, black, yellow, or brown race.

The totality of what we think is the totality of what we see as the world. We do not see a world outside thought because we are never silent, we are never without thought.

The movement of thought is the very movement of reality.

The projection of thought is the creation of a macro-thought that includes the thinker, a world outside the thinker, and a relationship between these two creations. This thinker–world relationship exists only in the thinking of it. It is the division of a universe, which is whole, into fragments. These fragments do not actually exist outside this thought process.

Due to the complexity of this thought-reality hologram, this projected world, we have come to believe in its reality. We believe it so fundamentally, that if this thought-reality is challenged, the challenge is automatically absorbed in the form of reaction.

The function of reaction is to protect the thought-reality, the "me," by negating the challenge. The negation of the challenge is accomplished simply by dividing once again the otherwise whole universe, and projecting the qualities which are challenged outward.

When confronted, we blame. When attacked, we counterattack. When questioned, we defend.

By blaming, reaction diverts attention from the "me" to the other. We can never take responsibility.

Our world, the world of "me," by its nature must be a divided world. As such, we can always find something outside of us which is responsible.

If, on the other hand, we are responsible for the entirety of our lives, if we have nothing "other" to blame, we are suddenly in a different universe. In this universe, we have no place to hide.

What disturbs us the most in the other is that which we have not completed in ourselves. This is simple to see in a psychological way, and we can observe this constantly in our daily lives.

This other that disturbs, this self that is disturbed, is not two things but one. The disturbance and the other are the projection of thought. Thought, rather than coming to its own cessation, its own quiet, divides itself. This divided, projected self, is a created world in which the "me" exists. This "me" is disturbed, and it is disturbed by the other.

Perhaps all of this is resolved with a new thought fragment, which we will call resolution. We create a problem, a disturbance, a conflict. Then we overlay a new idea, a solution. But, we are not resolved, we are just getting more complicated in our pain.

This is an incredibly complex dance of thought-reality, each moment face-to-face with the fact of emptiness, wholeness, and quiet. It is maintained by our inertia, our momentum, our habit. This frenetic fragmentation and reaction formation may take us into an increasingly disembodied state. Our energy, our identification becomes mentalized, disconnected from any physicality or interrelatedness.

This is insanity, madness. Thought has disembodied. It exists for its own perpetuation and within its own projection. This madness is now what is normal in our world.

If this kind of madness is normal, then what is normality?

If we understand this fragmentation of the world through the identification and projection of thought, what happens? Are we free and integrated in that understanding or does something else occur?

The understanding of the nature of thought takes place in a sudden insight, without context or cause. It may appear to be associated with a crisis, or collapse of some part of our life, a sudden death, a loss. This insight jars our perspective so thoroughly that we may lose our equilibrium entirely. We may lose our sense of solidity, our feeling of centeredness, our location as the viewer.

Now who are we? How do we function? How do we behave? If we are dislocated then where is it we are? Or are we at all?

This dislocation is our natural state. It might be thought of as normal. Yet, at this point we may be told that we are quite crazy.

The spiritual crisis that often accompanies insight into the actual nature of reality is usually recognized only as madness. The fragmentation that is the nature of identification with our thought is recognized only as normal. We have got it backwards. Those who are interested in viewing the nature of reality need understand this basic distortion and reversal of fact.

Because we have it backwards, there is generally no support in our world for this insight, dislocation, and integration. In fact, there can be no outer reference point, there is no madness, no normality. The basic movement of disintegration/integration is our nature.

The overlay of the consensus reality has defined the purpose of life in terms of productivity, material wealth, and macrosocial stability. Without this overlay, spiritual crisis is not experienced as an illness or dysfunction which needs to be cured. With this overlay, our natural state of disintegration/integration becomes an anathema in relation to mental health.

The materialism of this societal viewpoint attempts to suppress or modify this disintegration/integration. The result is functional, productive, stable citizenry without heart or soul, disembodied, fragmented, living, but without life, in a state of increasing despair.

Without the suppressive burden of the models of how to be, there is nothing to structure experience. Our experience laid bare is self-revelatory. We do not need interpretation. Without the burden of madness or the suppression of the natural state, integration is possible.

Integration is fully aware of the movement of thought-reality and does not object to it. It is not in conflict with the endless projection of thought, or the collective manifestation of thought-reality. Integration, because it is aware of the nature of thought-reality, knows that while reality appears to have substance, it is in fact empty. So, there is nothing to do about it, no reason to change it, or to object to it.

Integration is at rest in dislocation. It needs no place to reside. Its view is always spacious.

The integration of madness and normality is unconcerned with the norm because it has no location to compare, it is unable to be crazed because it is not in conflict with thought's projected reality.

Integration can communicate with, interact with the projected thought-reality. It inherently communicates because integration includes the space within which this thought-reality arises.

Integration is at rest.

Thought arises and passes away within the vastness of conscious space. From the vantage point of thought, there appears to be a crisis. From the vantage of space, there is silence. ✿

the collapse
of
self

AFTER MANY LONG sessions, the psychiatrist told his patient, "You're cured!"

"Big deal" said the patient, "When I came to you I was Napoleon. Now I'm nobody."

◌

THE STRUCTURE OF the self requires identification. Without the sense of being something, the idea of self collapses.

When we consider the collapse of the self, we think of insanity. And yet, we have seen that the normal state in which we have come to exist is quite insane in its nature. It is insane in its effect on our happiness and the quality of the life around us.

Is then the collapse of the idea of "me" our natural or normal state? Can life spontaneously move, without thought, without fragmentation, without memory and projection? Is there a functional requirement that we move from an identified center or ego?

The self defines itself in the positive by its position, accomplishments, identities, possessions. The self defines itself in the negative by its blame, its loss, the outside forces which affect it, hinder it, limit it, challenge it. This grinding friction between the positive and the negative is what gives the self its tactile reality.

Putting aside the identification with the positive and the reaction to the negative, what remains? There can be no description of a state that is not a state, that is without attributes. The quality of the conditioned self is understood in this moment. This realization comes without effort, with grace, with a kind of powerful emptiness.

There is nothing left but the expression of freedom.

We may penetrate to this deep understanding, but do we want a freedom which does not include our identity structure? Or do we want identification and blame? We may say that freedom is the obvious choice, but are we really prepared to give up the positive and negative identification? Are we prepared for the collapse of the self?

When we consider the collapse of the self, fear arises. This fear projects the world as it will be after our identity collapses, a world of confusion, disarray, and pain. This is ironic since this is not the world that we will be in, but rather the world that, in fact, we are in now.

If we stop the forward momentum of our habitual, repetitive self, who will we be, what will we do? We fear the loss of identification, family, friends, and job. We do not know what the world will look like without our current structures.

Perhaps what we should actually fear is the continuation of these structures. If there is something to be afraid of it is that we will pass through our life without understanding our identifications, without true communication with our family, without finding the depths of friendship, without a purposeful function. This prospect is truly terrifying.

We accept our desperate lives as a trade-off for the security of the known. There is nothing more secure than a prison. Our personal solitary confinement, the confinement of the "me," is our prison's ultimate refuge.

Outside the walls of our prison is the unknown. It is not secure, but it is free.

We do not know what is outside the walls of the prison of our mind, because we have never ventured there. While our fear projects what is there, it cannot know. Fear cannot leave the prison because it must always guard its inmates.

But, if the self collapses, if the walls come down, is it fear that remains, or is it freedom? ❧

love,

emptiness,

and energy

WE OFTEN FEEL that we are not loved enough. This is a reflection of the fact that we do not love, that we cannot find our capacity to love.

Love is not something that we do to one another. There is no object or subject in love.

Love is what is present when there is no object–subject, when there are not two.

This feeling of not being loved is in fact the need for love, the need for a cessation of the divided world in which our egos exist.

This cessation does not come about through someone loving us.

It does not come about by us loving another.

Love is not causal. It cannot be created, it cannot be practiced, it cannot be taught.

We can deeply inspect what we are, and in that we can see the structure of division which is inherent to thought, memory, and ego. We can cease. We can be still.

Love, which is the very energy and expression of life, is whole. Thought cannot approach this energy. Words cannot capture it.

This energy of wholeness cannot be used, or divided, or squandered.

It is us all, and all of us.

This is not the answer to our question, it is the question fallen silent.

Having seen the nature of our thought and ego, we may pass through this gateway into silence.

We have left a world of fragments, and entered into something which is whole, but is empty. If there is no namer, then there are no names. If there is no subject, there is no object. This is emptiness.

There is tremendous energy here because there is nothing to dissipate it. There is great creativity, because there is nothing to restrict it.

Though the psychological self, the ego-center has gone silent, there is nothing lost. Out of this vast expansion of quiet, the energy of life expresses.

The nature of this energy, because it is beyond cause and effect, is unknown. It cannot be contained by concept, or manipulated by thought or used in any way.

We are not the experiencers or explorers of this energy. We are this energy: expressing, exploring, manifesting, and disintegrating. ❦

communication
beyond
language

WE MUST BE vigilant that the very consideration of the nature of consciousness and reality does not generate more concepts, more philosophy, more conditioning.

It is with this caveat that these words must be read. This is not an investigation which is for the casually interested, the partly committed, the intellectually stimulated.

These words only have value, particularly words referring to something which is inherently beyond language, if we deeply reflect upon them in the actuality of our life.

Words become a trap without this fundamental inspection of our own thought structure. Words become empowered by the spontaneous quiet which appears when thought is in abeyance.

There is no need for any new ideology, but there is an urgent need for each of us to discover the truth of our existence—firsthand. This self-discovery cannot be instructed. It must arise of its own necessity.

Yet, upon finding this movement of self-discovery occurring, it is incumbent that we communicate. This need to communicate arises directly from the recognition of our basic connection with all that is around us. Communication is inherent to that recognition. We have no choice.

This communication may be through words, or deeds, or silence. The form will not be important, so long as this communication is not ideology or an attempt to condition another. Communication is not the conveyance of an idea from one to another, but rather the conveyance of silence.

Communication is not from a position. It is not from knowledge speaking to ignorance. Communication does not result in power, followers, or organizations.

Communication is the anointment of freedom, the benediction of love.

Whatever understanding we may come to in our lives, it is not solely for our benefit. Our discovery is meaningful only in relationship, of which communication is the expression.

Communication, which has come to refer to words, has its roots of meaning in the qualities of giving to another, of imparting, of transmission.

The word communication shares its roots with communion, an act of sharing, and community which is a unified body of individuals.

If communication is the expression of relationship, then what is the form of this expression? How do we actually communicate, give, impart, and transmit?

Answering this question is the active experiment in which each of us is absorbed. The forms we find in our world do not now reflect community, communion, and communication.

The expression of relationship, which is communication, sharing, love, needs to find form. This movement to form is the transformation of the body, the family, the society, and the world. Can this movement take place, this radical shift, without the projection of thought, concept, or ideology capturing and distorting it?

This question, while asked universally, is most pertinent when applied to us directly, individually, in the practicality of our actual lives. If we are seeking the security of ideology, if we are functioning out of a survival modality, if we live in separation from the world around us, then this shift has already found resistance.

It is not the world that needs to change, we must change. It is not the world which is too complex, we are. Politicians, priests, and corporations do not hold back a humane, compassionate world, we do.

We are the politicians in our everyday negotiations and dishonesties as we buy friendship, marriage, and family with compromise. We are the priests as we ritualize our lives, as we refuse to examine the concepts and images by which we live. We are the corporations because we pollute, we are wasteful, we are greedy, so that we will be secure and profit in our lives at the expense of others.

Let us stop. We do not need to do it this way.

By understanding the nature of our connectivity, we also discover that the problem and the solution dissolve in this realization.

Now our actions arise spontaneously, without fear, without separation. We begin to move through our life without thought projected out of memory, out of the depth of silence. This movement is whole, it comes from and returns to that which is common. This is communication, communion, and community.

There is a very simple discovery that we may make as we investigate the nature of our world. This discovery is that while it may appear that we are just in the world, in fact, we find that we are the world.

We can no longer find absolute points of separation from what we experience around us. We discover that our movement affects what appears to be around us, and what appears to be around us affects us. Like the quantum physicist's inseparability of objects, we discover we affect and are affected by elements of our world which appear to be distinct and different.

Inherent to this communication, this flowing back and forth of energy, this expression of love is the discovery that we are not separate from anything. Far from being the end of the story, this is really more the beginning. ℂ

the challenge
of
living

RECOGNIZING OURSELVES as the world is also recognizing ourselves in the world. This fundamental contact does not allow for a psychological or physical withdrawal. There is no cave, no space away, no quiet and controlled viewpoint in which to hide.

This contact is the beginning of the transformation of the elemental world in all its forms. The contact with the world is not with an intention of changing it into something else. This contact with the world *is* change. Consciousness contacting reality alters it. Awareness contacting thought changes it.

What does all of this mean regarding our day-to-day lives? We have seen that our thoughts have created our self, that this self is fiction and that we function from and about this fiction.

Yet, we still find ourselves faced with questions of livelihood, money, relationship, sex, politics, community, family.

∽

SEEKING TO AVOID just such issues, a man once decided to simplify his life and dedicate it to the discovery of the eternal. He gave up everything and sat under a tree to contemplate the universe. His only possession was the loincloth he wore. Admirers and disciples came, of course.

One day he discovered a rat was chewing on his loincloth and he asked his disciples what to do.

"You must get a cat to keep away the rat," he was advised.

And so he got a cat.

But, the cat would not stay, so again the disciples were asked for advice.

"The cat will only stay if you give it milk. You must get a cow for milk."

And so the ascetic got a cow. But the cow needed to be grazed. So he got a servant to graze the cow. But the servant wanted his family nearby, so the family came to stay. They needed a house to live in. And the cow became a small herd to support the family.

And so the ascetic soon forgot his simple life and his contemplation of the universe—all because of a simple loincloth.

༄

WE CANNOT AVOID our own materiality, even by realizing its limitation. Does the deep realization of our nature address the functions of our life? Does it pay the rent? Buy our food? Pay the bills?

If not, then what does? How does money flow into and out of our lives? And, what is money, after all?

Money is a great taboo, particularly if we consider ourselves as spiritual. We are either suffering from a lack of it or burdened by an excess of it. We are attached to money out of fear, out of our need for security. We cannot deal with money because we cannot deal with our fear. We cling to our money habits in desperation. We seek experts to advise us, to instruct us, to cure us of our money fear and our money love.

༄

A MAN WENT to the psychiatrist who declared that the man's problem was that he was too attached to material things.

"Can you cure me?" asked the man.

"Sure," said the psychiatrist, "That'll be $500."

ꙮ

IT IS SIMPLE to come up with aphorisms about money. Books are sold by the millions that teach people how to be "money machines," how to "attract money," how to be a "money magnet" and so forth. The authors of these books prove their point by their own example, by selling the books. They do not understand money, they understand greed.

Even the experts on money appear terrified of it. Bertrand Russell once said that "you could lay all the economists in the world end-to-end without reaching a conclusion." The experts are like priests performing prognostic rituals.

Greed *is* the answer for our individual wants, separated from the world around us. But if we cease to believe in the "me," then we cease to believe in greed.

What moves us to money when we are not acting from greed, from fear?

What kind of job will we go to, what kind of business will we create, what kind of organization will we become when this movement is not from fear and greed? Isn't it clear that without acting from a center, everything we touch, everything we do, is changed? Profound quiet enters the workplace in such a way that our work is not making widgets, or selling widgets, or speculating in widget futures—our work becomes this profound quiet.

If this profound quiet is indeed what we are about, the detail of what we do, the actual work or activity, becomes a reflection of that quality. This quality of quiet becomes the milieu in which we function.

Now what becomes most evident to us is not the quiet and the reflection of that quiet in our work, but the impingements on that quiet expression. Because quiet has become the norm, conflict becomes the exception. If there is conflict in our work, if there is stress, if there is damage, then this will be underscored.

Since this quiet is our work, what is conflicted at our work must come to resolution, or the work changes. When this quiet and care is so important to us, when this quality is the central concern of our life, we cannot continue with activity which is destructive or devitalizing. We cannot damage ourselves for money, we cannot damage another. Fundamental quiet is not possible at a bomb factory.

We may come to understand how much of our work is not about order, contact, and stillness. We may see how much is about competition, power and position, fear, survival.

Psychological time, which is memory projected, which is future and past, drives our work because it drives money. "Time is money," is an aphorism which has become an accepted concept. We work for a future where we are too old to work, but we will still need money. We work because the rent or mortgage is due, or groceries must be bought once more. This fear of lack in the future drives us, just as it has for thousands of years.

But, if our work is profound quiet, there is no beginning or end to our workday, there is no retirement and there is no future or past.

Is there good pay and a benefits package for this work of profound quiet, this stepping out of time and future and fear?

The fact is that the pay is just enough, not more. Just enough may not be what we expect, or want, or dream of, nevertheless, it is enough.

This is not "prosperity consciousness," this is not "creating your own reality," this does not sell books and feed fantasies. Just enough may be more radical simplicity than we ever considered, but enough is a response to our life, not to our greed, self-centeredness, cravings, and compulsions.

If we want to satisfy our greed and compulsions, we must abandon the quiet, where enough is sufficient, and we must reenter the world of thought and division. There, we can manipulate reality, bending it to our material desires. This can be done easily. We can create wealth, prosperity. We hope that we can acquire more and more, until we are full. Then we will be done, then we will have it all.

But, we can never be full, we can only consume. We have forgotten that we are empty, we have forgotten that self cannot be filled because it does not exist in actuality. The self can only consume, it can never be full, it can never come to rest.

Recognizing this, we may see our needs differently. We actually have enough and need nothing more than just enough. Our actual requirements are really just to be still, to love, to relate.

The pay for the recognition of this fundamental quiet is just enough. Not a great deal, but all things considered, a fair deal. After all, there is just enough for all of us, no one need be left out.

In the same way our relationship to money and work is conditioned, the social expression, the organization of our family, education, and government is also conditioned. The social expression is a form of macroconditioning. These are large-scale patterns of behavior that are the sum of a multitude of conditioned thoughts.

Because these forms have evolved over long periods of time, they tend to exist without challenge as the unconscious backdrop of our lives.

If we begin to question the nature of self, we also begin to question the entirety of the social structure.

What happens to this structure when deeply questioned? Are we willing to live in a way which is not controlled by these forms?

What occurs if the basis for intimacy is not reproduction, the basis for continuity in relationship is not religious marriage, the basis for community association is not survival, and the basis for political organization is not defense or security?

Can we even imagine such a life? In fact, we can see some of this occurring as our world rapidly changes. But this change is unconscious. The forms which come from this change will reflect the same underlying fear that has driven form in the past.

Traditional marriage has begun to break down as birth control, the dissipation of religion, and the pressures of contemporary life combine to create serial monogamy as a substitute for marriage. Where has marriage come from? Where has monogamy come from? How have these forms become accepted and protected? Is some other form emerging?

Relationship is not two negotiating their relative positions, possessions, and psychology. Relationship is the sharing of a deep examination of the nature of our world. This sharing, this relationship, cannot be limited to our wives or husbands. It must, by its nature, include all who wish to be included.

We may feel that we have just one other who is willing to walk with us on this journey, but this is not a statement of some natural law. Our society, our education, our religion may reinforce this notion.

But if our intimacy is with just one other, hasn't our isolation, our loneliness, our fear simply expanded to include two?

If relationship is the recognition of a shared life, then this recognition cannot stop at any boundary whatever.

If there is no boundary, then we begin to question all the assumptions we have, all the assumptions we have been given about relationship.

Marriage is not made strong by isolating and focusing our feeling of love on one person. This is the seed of its destruction, the end of its vitality, either the death of the marriage or else the death in the marriage.

Marriage instead can be an amplification of love and freedom. This requires two people who are free and do not contain their love within the boundaries of a single relationship.

Community, which is now based on the mutual protection of possessions, territory, property, is unraveling. Can community be based on something else?

෴

THE STUDENT WENT to the mystic and begged to be shown the difference between Heaven and Hell.

The mystic, finally relenting, took the student down deep into the bowels of the universe to the realm of Hell.

There the student saw people sitting around a huge circular table, each with a six-foot-long spoon that could just reach a vast pot of stew. The stew was the most marvelous of stews and the very smell of it brought delight to the perceiver.

But the people, doomed to Hell, could not bring the spoons to their mouth as they were far too long. The people of Hell were in agony. They were unable to feed themselves. They were starving.

The student was awed, but still had not seen Heaven.

The mystic took the student through the expanses of the cosmos until they reached the realm of Heaven.

There the student saw the same immense round table with people sitting around it, the same marvelous stew, and the very same six-foot-long spoons in everyone's hands.

Only, in Heaven everyone was happy and laughing—as they fed each other.

ᕲ

IF WE LOOK to the very core of our being, the basis of these social structures, can something new emerge?

If we do nothing to stop it, community naturally expresses from our lives. It is inherent to our humanness. It is the representation of the fact of our connectedness.

What we do to stop ourselves from community is myriad. Every concept we cling to divides us, every fear we identify with divides us.

We accept an ever-smaller subdivision of life as our community. We embody that shrinking world in our faceless housing unit, our gliding automobile with tinted windows, our communication through computer and telephone. This is the expression of isolation, fear, and pain.

We have stopped ourselves from communing. Why?

Community requires a radical simplification of our lives. When our focus becomes our inherent relatedness, not survival, then what we do with our lives and how we do it drastically changes.

The expression of community is the reflection of our collective realization. It is important to our children that they have loving parents. It is just as important that there is a loving community to receive them as they come into this life.

If we are to raise children, we must also raise communities. If not, our children will continue to be patterned in the isolation we have come to accept in our contemporary societies.

These new communities can be free of ideology, and instead be based on the direct perception of relationship. How will decisions be made? How will money be kept or distributed? What is ownership? How will the young be educated? How will the sick and the old be cared for? The exploration of questions such as these forms the basis of such a community. Like the view of life itself, such a community will always be moving, changing, and self-revealing.

Part of the community function must be to help those around us who live in need. Often our view of helping is clouded by our ideas about what helping is.

While living in need may be most obviously expressed by the absence of food and shelter, poverty is most directly understood as the loss of contact with our relatedness. This contraction and cutting off from life and life's sustenance is the basic structure of destitution, which is reinforced by the outer circumstance of material poverty.

We may fulfill the material needs of the other, but we can only truly address that person's needs if we also address the person. We may give someone food, we may even teach them to farm.

But, this is not enough to address the poverty. The response is not deep enough.

To find the response that is complete, we must go to the depths of our own being. It is much easier to give money and to feel for a moment that we have given, we have done something, we feel something.

There really is no such thing as giving, because there is no such thing as having. We may be the custodians of the wealth which accumulates in our life, but we certainly do not own it. We will all leave this life empty-handed.

Our infatuation with the goodness of giving drives much of our imagined altruism. We feel good by doing good. But, does feeling good mean that we are doing good? If we do not actually have anything and cannot give, consequently, we are stripped of the pleasure of giving. What then will drive our charity?

Distribution to those in need is one of our primary functions in life, and it is one of our basic needs. The giver needs to give. It is our need to give because it is our need to be in full relationship with the life around us. By giving relationship, we receive relationship.

Relationship demands that there be an intelligence to our charity. This intelligence discerns that giving to one who does not need is not a gift. Giving to one who has the capacity to be self-supporting is destructive. In such a situation, communication, not giving, is the fact of relationship. Is the helper prepared to put aside the role of charity in order to point out the capacity of the individual to help themselves? Or, are we too wrapped up in being good?

And what happens to the humanness of the ones who truly do not have the capacity to help themselves when we help them? We must not only assist them with their material needs, but more importantly, enter into relationship with them. Giving without relationship creates an object out of a human being. It is possible to be fed, but to starve. The response to this spiritual starvation is our primary giving.

No amount of food and shelter will solve the human condition. Our condition is a result of our

view, our mind, our illusion. Our responsibility to
help is the responsibility to relate. In relationship,
we discover that the divisions that thought creates
dissolve into wholeness. ℭ

health,
disease,
and aging

THE BODY IS the meeting point of consciousness and reality, energy and matter, silence and mind. Because it is the point of meeting, it is neither of these qualities and both of them. Perhaps it is more accurate to think of the body as an energy transformer.

Physicists use the term "wave of probability" to describe the smallest elements of matter. These elements have quantifiable existence only upon observation. Until the point of observation, they have tendencies or probabilities, but no actuality.

The apparently purely physical nature of the body diminishes as we closely observe ourselves. We begin to see that there is a psychic and a somatic aspect, but that neither can be isolated from the other.

We can alter our physical state through application of mental focus, such as suggestion, stress, visualization and perhaps a multitude of placebo effects. We can alter our mental states through application of physical elements, such as drugs, food, and physical trauma.

With this in consideration, it becomes obvious that great care must be taken with our diet, exercise, and exposure to environmental influences of all types. No book can tell us precisely how to be healthy, what to eat, how to exercise. But, our bodies can tell us this. Each of these parts impacts the totality of our psychosomatic condition, which in turn may affect our receptivity to the whole of life.

Upon deeper reflection, we may also come to understand that the nature of disease and aging in the body is the movement of thought as memory. This memory may be encoded in the genetic makeup, in the culture of medical practice, in the mental and physical habituations in which we live.

Thought, as memory, perpetuates itself, and in this way we can see that our body, our disease, our aging is an expression of this memory.

No system of health nor scientific advance has had any profound impact on the eradication of disease or aging. We have "conquered" certain disease formations, but new diseases have appeared. We have extended our life span through technology, but have found that life extension is accompanied by loneliness, depression, mental incapacity, and continued deterioration of the body. Death is still a fact. It is simply delayed.

We view the body as a mechanical system. The biochemical models of our bodies are mechanical in nature. Doctors are rigorously schooled in biology, biochemistry, and physics. This is only a small part of the picture.

Even with the recent inclusion of Eastern medical models and techniques, we still view the body mechanically. We know this is an incomplete viewpoint, we know there are phenomena which science cannot explain. We know that the placebo effect is unexplained, yet accepted. We know that our medical models are based on statistical results, that our cures or therapies are often simply statistically significant, but not understood.

Our medical diagnosis is determining probability, not fact. The doctor gathers information on symptoms. Through the analysis of the statistical probability of a symptom relating to a particular disease, diagnosis is made. Computer systems now replicate this function, they are in use at medical schools and they use eighteenth-century statistical theory to diagnose. The program simply adjusts the odds as more information is gathered, until the probability is that a particular disease is present.

A similar machine, or doctor, can dispense the medicine which has a statistically significant probability of relieving the symptoms.

Who is the patient in this nexus of symptom probability/cure probability? Isn't the patient viewed as a probability wave like the quantum physicists' unobserved matter?

Doesn't the viewer change that probability into matter, the human being into a concretized symptom-cure complex, simply by the fact of viewing, that is, diagnosing?

Quantum physics describes some elements of a new medical paradigm. The subatomic universe is a world where nothing has inherent location or physicalness without the application of observation. This observation alters the probable world into a definite world.

The effect of observation is that possibility becomes actualized. Which possibility, however, is not predictable. Physicists maintain that the actualization of reality in the subatomic world is completely random. Randomness creates patterns, however, which begin to look intelligent. Mathematicians expect that a monkey typing randomly on a keyboard will, given sufficient time, create the complete works of Shakespeare. What is the true creative power of randomness given endless time?

The subatomic universe is described as existing without location, inseparable and without objective nature. This farthest edge of science begins to look like the world described by mystics.

If quantum physics describes a mystical world, how is it that our medical model is so mechanical, so devoid of the spiritual? To answer this question, we must look at the history of physics.

Newton published his *Principia Mathematica* in 1687, just a few years after the dodo bird became extinct. Newton's work was significant because it laid the groundwork for the gross prediction and manipulation of the material world. Almost as an aside, it ushered in a materialistic and mechanical view of the universe.

In fact, Newton's laws of physics were intellectual marvels. But the absorption of these principles and their amplification by those who came after Newton created a view of the universe which was without soul, without spirit, without godhead.

Newton proved materialism and the mechanical nature of the universe. The Newtonian world was a cause-and-effect world. It was quantifiable, measurable, and predictable. But, Newton was wrong. He forgot one thing: the observer. Different observers of a phenomenon (such as the speed of light) meant different observations and suddenly the absolute was relative.

Einstein noticed this and quite a few other problems with Newtonian physics and, in the early part of the twentieth century, began publishing theories relating to vast movements of the physical world—the speed of light, gravity, and time. Einstein told us that time is relative. He gave us the famous Twins Paradox, which says that if one twin is rocketed off into space at sufficient velocity, he will return to earth younger than the twin that stayed behind. If time is relative, then the further question became, what is time?

Now physicists talked about four-dimensional space-time, time slowing down or speeding up, the relativity of the very world that Newton had described. The absolute world of Newton was now the relative world of Einstein.

But, even Einstein was not ready for the next development in physics: the world of quantum physics.

As profound as the shift from the absolute mechanical world of Newton to the relative world of Einstein was, the shift to the quantum physical world was even more radical. Einstein had forgotten one thing, and it is fascinating that he did. That one thing is consciousness.

Physicists had discovered that their very presence—that is the presence of consciousness—profoundly affected the quantifiable reality they were observing.

Physicist John Wheeler put it most succinctly when he wrote, "What philosophy suggested in times past, the central feature of quantum mechanics tells us today with impressive force. In some strange sense, this is a participatory universe."

Physicist Eugene Wigner writes, "It was not possible to formulate the laws of quantum mechanics in a fully consistent way without references to consciousness."

Including the field of consciousness in the world of physics brings us to some radical and fascinating notions. For example, what is the effect of consciousness on measurable, quantifiable subatomic phenomena? Physicist Werner Heisenberg suggested that in the subatomic world you could not observe a phenomenon without changing it. Further, he noted that while some part of a subatomic particle can be measured, for example, momentum, its position could not be measured at the same time. The picture, in a sense, would always be fuzzy. He wrote, "The atoms and elementary particles . . . form a world of potentialities or possibilities rather than one of things or facts."

He described an unobserved or unconscious phenomenon as a "probability wave" or "tendency for something."

"It introduces something standing in the middle, between the idea of an event and the actual event, a strange kind of physical reality just in the middle between possibilities."

Meanwhile, Irish physicist John Stuart Bell showed in what has become known as Bell's Theorem that any two atoms, once having encountered each other, will forever be connected or have an influence on each other, regardless of their location or distance from each other. This universal connectivity is outside the realm of cause and effect. Physicists consider cause/effect to be bounded by the speed of light. The effect Bell describes is superluminal—faster than the speed of light.

The implication of Bell's Theorem is profound. It implies what the mystic states: the universe is connected, there is no true separation, what occurs here may instantly have an effect on there. Bell's work indicates an effect that is outside of causation, outside of process, outside of time. It indicates a quality which is described by science, but cannot be explained by science. Science has gone past its own understanding.

What this farthest edge of science is describing is the very early and rudimentary scientific contact with consciousness. And as we have seen, consciousness fundamentally alters everything it touches. The scientific paradigm is being transformed, and with this change comes an expansion of the possibilities that science accepts.

The quantum physical world is far more than the collective calculations of a few brilliant but isolated scientists. It is, in fact, the beginning of a scientific description of this new paradigm. It is the beginning of a description of a world in which consciousness affects reality, where the change in one point in the universe changes the entire universe, where reality itself is not in existence without the contact with consciousness.

Newtonian physics, and its inherent materialism, was a wrong turn that it took us 300 years to discover. In those centuries, the Newtonian view was absorbed into our worldview. It permeated every aspect of our reality. It told us, counterintuitively, that the world was mechanical and predictable.

In those same centuries, we developed scientific principles that corresponded to this materialism. Out of this grew our medicine, our psychiatry, our view of time, aging, and ultimately death. In the Newtonian world, these are all mechanical, predictable, material.

The new paradigm of relativity and the quantum physical reality has not been absorbed. In part, it has not even been formulated by the scientists, let alone integrated by the general culture.

This new paradigm, a mutable, interconnected universe transformed by consciousness, has been realized, formulated, and expressed for thousands of years. It is the realization of mystics. It has been described in the Vedas of the Hindus, the Kabbalah of Judaism, the teachings of the Sufis, the Christian mystics, and the Taoist sages. As science finally recognizes mysticism as its own, the shift of view, the shift of consciousness will change our medical reality.

In that shift, we may see the application of consciousness to the challenges of health and disease. Only recently has mainstream medicine recognized the intuitively obvious: that relaxation affects heart health, that visualization affects immune function, that the repetition of sound or mantras affects blood pressure and other body systems, that prayer heals.

This is just the crude beginning of the application of consciousness to the alteration of apparently physical systems. Conscious patterning of health is the unlimited potential of humanity—once we become conscious.

In fact, we may discover that consciousness *is* health. Does this natural state of awareness, by its innate nature, pattern reality in an inherently balanced way? Does consciousness age? Does it die?

Science knows little about the attributes of consciousness. Only archetype and mythology have attempted to describe the conscious universe, in which exist the answers to the mysteries of disease, aging, and death. But, each of us has the capacity to connect myth and science, physics and metaphysics, the material and the mystic. This connection is our birthright. It is the very nature of existence.

Reality only exists at this meeting point and because of this meeting point. We are both the expression of consciousness and the embodiment of it in the materiality.

Consciousness without the material has no expression, the material without consciousness has no reality. Neither has existence in actuality without the other.

Because we are each at the nexus of this consciousness–material interface, we have access to both aspects. While we have understood a great deal about the manipulation of the material, we have not learned enough about the nature of consciousness. While our knowledge of science, the description of the material world, fills great libraries, we do not have even a working theory of consciousness.

Yet, as we have seen, physicists have discovered that consciousness, when in contact with the material world, profoundly changes it. This change is outside of time. It is not a process.

Consciousness, which is directly accessible to each of us, profoundly changes us. That change is outside of time. It is not a process.

What is the effect of consciousness on disease? Does it profoundly change the disease complex? We each have access to consciousness, there is nothing which limits our research.

When we fall ill, what is our state of consciousness? Can we stop our busyness, can we stop our schedule, our habits, and find consciousness? What occurs in that moment of stopping, of doing nothing, of contact with the energy of life?

The resistance to stopping, to quiet, to contact with the life energy is the disease process itself. The body needs consciousness, life energy. It is starving. Disease is the starvation of the body. The starvation is not for food but for the entry of consciousness into the very cells of the body.

This chronic consciousness-starvation is manifest in the slow decline and degeneration of the physical body. It is the disease process. It is the aging process, mechanically imprinted in our memory, our genes. It is the relentless march to disintegration of the physical and the ultimate merger of the physical with the life energy.

We age because we are told to do so, we *remember* to do so, as an expression of our most fundamental biomemory, our genetic code.

But, must we age? Many life-forms regenerate. Some simple life-forms are virtually immortal. What is the effect of consciousness on the aging process, on the encoded memory of the genetic material?

Death itself becomes a question in the face of consciousness. What occurs when death is confronted with consciousness?

This quantum/mystical/magical universe has the potential for eradication of disease, aging, and death. This universe already exists and we are already in it. We are simply conditioned by thousands of years of linear thought. This thought cannot fathom a nonlinear, nonsolid, timeless, mutable universe. Concrete thought cannot imagine a universe of pure energy which manifests through its own inherent intelligence.

The potential for the eradication of disease, aging, and death lies in the merger of the psychosomatic plexus, in which we are embodied, with an entirely new and unconditioned energy. This energy, free from the constraints of thought, is also free from memory. This energy entered into the psychosomatic conditioning, thereby transforming it, may be the next evolutionary leap.

We know very little about this energy. Many have attempted to bring this into the physical over the ages—mystics, shamans, alchemists, physicists. We see only fragments of its nature in spontaneous remissions, psychic phenomenon, miraculous healings, and perhaps in examples of revival of some clinically dead. We have seen the fragments of its nature in the arcane experiments of the physicist and the calculations of the mathematicians.

These fragments show us the possibility that life energy can move in ways that do not fit our scientific or cultural paradigms.

Because we are so cluttered with concepts and ideologies, we cannot approach this undivided energy. We can only theorize about its potential in actualizing the human body. But, theory will do little good.

We do not know yet what is necessary to bring this quality into the very cells of our being. First, let us strip away what is known, and then perhaps we will discover what is beyond. What is beyond is what is possible. ☙

death
and
immortality

DEATH IS NOT at the end of our lives. Death is current. It is now.

Death comes in the passing away of thought, in the dissolution of self. Death is the very essence of life, it is not different than life.

There is no place that you can find, no point, no view that is not dying the moment you find it.

There is no birth that does not already contain death as its expression.

There is no death which does not bring about the new.

Do we live to cling to what is dying, or nurture what is new?

In the moment we die, in each moment we die, what is new is waiting to express.

From the vantage of life, which is continuous, uninterrupted by the flow of form coming into being and passing away, there is no death. There is only life which is the timeless expression of its own innate nature.

When our view is from the vantage of that timeless expression, we, too, are timeless, immortal. We have died in that view. We are no longer separate. ℭ

inquiry

LIFE IS DYNAMIC. It is changing, moving.

Because we risk becoming dogmatic and conceptualized in our life, it is important to push at the edges of our understanding.

Realization of the absolute is not the end, but the beginning of inquiry into that absolute.

Recognizing the limitation of the conditioned state is not the end of the state. Our question becomes the investigation of that conditioned state, and its transformation.

This integration of the absolute and the relative, the conditioned and the unconditioned, is a kind of evolution of consciousness which is taking place in all of us, but which is taking place outside of time.

We believe we can easily retreat into the cave of our understanding in a kind of spiritual smugness. We believe that there we will see the nature of reality and of absolute consciousness without hindrance or challenge.

We cannot actually retreat anywhere, because the nature of reality and absolute consciousness is what we retreat from and where we retreat to. It is everything and everywhere.

Can that realization come into our everyday life? Can the workplace, the community, the home be transformed? Can the body itself undertake the transmutation necessary for it to be the vehicle for this energy, for it to be this energy, rather than the expression of disease, aging, and death?

This is the inquiry into life, into every nook and cranny of our existence. We do not know where this movement is directed. We do know that without this our world continues as a place of apparent conflict.

It is uncertain whether the world can survive the continued fragmentation of war, politics, overpopulation, and pollution. It is certain, however, that without a radical change in the very structure and basis for our collective lives, nothing but more of the same can occur.

The conflict, we discover, is not out there. The end of conflict, the discovery of the fundamental mutation of the entirety of our existence, begins with us. Responsibility is not elsewhere.

The relatedness, and the exploration of the world of relationship, takes its form and structure from wholeness. This movement can only take place without us, that is, without the psychological "me."

This movement, without a center, yet probing and changing every aspect of our lives, is the meeting of energy and matter, consciousness and reality. It is the unknown lover come to call. ℣

invitation

to

a dialogue

THIS IS AN INVITATION to a dialogue. This dialogue may take many forms. Dialogue is the unifying expression of duality. It is the one embrace of
the apparent two.

The totality of life is inclusive of all forms
and, recognizing this, form attempts to see the
formless in the other.

This is not the dominance of one over the
other, or the instruction of one to the other. This
dialogue is inclusive of the other.

It may be the inspection of the inner and the
outer. It may be a dialogue with our wife, our hus-
band, our child, our friend. It may be the unex-
pected meeting on a busy street, the beauty of a

newly opened flower, the empathetic response to someone's pain. It is the dialectic of life with itself.

We are all part of this vast conversation, the play of life in its apparent parts and its undeniable oneness. As we converse, let us find our way back to the point of our conversation, the beginning of our play with ourselves.

When we speak to each other, let us recognize that we are speaking to ourselves. When we meet each other, we are not meeting a stranger, we have simply forgotten that we have already met, already conversed so many times. This is the dialogue.

Let us invite this dialogue in our lives. ℒ